POETRY PROMPTS

All sorts of ways to start a poem
from **JOSEPH COELHO**

Illustrated by **Georgie Birkett**, **Grasya Oliyko**,
Amanda Quartey and **Viola Wang**

WIDE EYED EDITIONS

CONTENTS

INTRODUCTION

You might not realise it but you are a poet! You became a poet as soon as you opened this book because you started a journey. Your adventure through these pages will show you how to create all sort of poems about all sort of things: poems about animals, poems about emotions, poems that you can write on plastic bottles and stones, poems that can be whispered and poems that will have you using your voice in lots of fun and creative ways.

When I was a kid, poetry didn't just help me to imagine and create new worlds and characters. It also showed me a fun, positive way to express my feelings, emotions and experiences. I hope that the 41 poetry prompts in this book will help you discover the poet within! When you're ready I hope that you will share these poems, read them to a friend, perform them to your class or school, put them up on a display board or simply stick them up on your fridge. Poems come to life when they are shared and I hope you will get as much fun sharing your wonderful poems as I have had sharing mine within these pages.

As you start to put pen to paper, remember that you are the boss! There is no right or wrong in a poem, it's up to you whether you use rhyme, don't use rhyme, make your poem long or short, make it funny, sad, serious or just plain silly. These prompts are here to help you discover that a poem can be many things. Good luck on your poetry adventure with the Poetry Prompts.

A NOTEBOOK OF YOUR OWN

Having **a notebook of your own** is very important as a writer.
I always have mine nearby. I even keep it by my bed, so that if an idea
or a poem comes at night, I can stick it in my book. Carry yours with
you wherever you go: you never know when an idea for a poem might hit!

I'm going to show you how you can make a mini notebook
of your own. All you need is one sheet of paper:

You can give your mini notebook a front cover, and a title and fill it
with any poems or ideas you like. When it's full you can get a new sheet
of paper and make another. You could create a whole library of your ideas!

Now that you have a mini notebook of your own, you can put
some mini poems inside. Why not have a go at the next
exercise and fill a few pages with some one word poems?

ONE WORD POEMS

Did you know that you can write a poem with just **one word**? Well, you can! There is a trick to it, the trick is to have a long title.

Here is my title:

The Happy Tale Of A Panda

and my one word for this poem is...

The Happy Tale Of A Panda
Bamboo!

Let's think of another using a different title:

The Day I Was Swallowed By My Bed

What would your one word be for that title? Mine would be...

The Day I Was Swallowed By My Bed
Dreams!

Have a go at thinking of your own one word poem titles. You can base them on mine above or make them totally different.

POETRY POWER-UP

If you would like more of a challenge you can write lots of one word poems all about the same theme and link them together to make a longer poem, like this:

The Sound Of Water
Splash.

The Feel Of Water
Cold.

The Taste Of Water
Nothing.

I aM PoeM

Let's create **a poem all about us**, about ourselves and how wonderful we are. The poem will end up a bit like this...

I am the claws of a tiger
because I get to the point.

I am the wings of a bird
because I take flight.

I am the fur of a chinchilla
because I'm super-soft.

There is a pattern is this poem, did you notice it?

I am the *SOMETHING* of a *SOMETHING* because...

Easy, right? All you have to do is fill in the gaps with your own ideas to create your poem.
I am the ___ of a ___
because ___.

POETRY POWER-UP

Think about all the things that make you great and add them to your verses. Here is my powered-up poem!

I am the claws of a tiger
because I get to the point.
I am organised and sharp.

I am the wings of a bird
because I take flight.
Flying through the skies
of my imagination.

I am the fur of a chinchilla
because I'm super-soft.
I try to be kind and friendly
to all.

FUN WITH RHYMES

Rhyme gives a poem instant rhythm.
Let's write a **nonsense rhyming poem**.

1. Start by choosing two words that you want to rhyme with.
I'm going to choose NIGHT and BEAR.

2. Next make two lists of words that rhyme with NIGHT and BEAR....

NIGHT	BEAR
Sight	Care
Flight	Stare
Light	Lair

3. Now turn the words into sentences with one
of the rhyming words at the end.

The stars are shining in the sky at NIGHT.
Shooting stars are out of SIGHT.
I feel like a drone taking FLIGHT.
The sun is shining with its warm LIGHT.

I feel snug under the covers with my teddy BEAR.
I fall deeply asleep without a CARE.
When I turn the corner everyone stops to STARE.
I am a dragon curled up in her LAIR.

Now I am going to muddle these sentences up.

I feel snug in bed with my teddy BEAR.
The stars are shining in the sky at NIGHT.
I fall deeply asleep without a CARE.
Shooting stars are out of SIGHT.

When I turn the corner everyone stops to STARE.
I feel like a drone taking FLIGHT.
A dragon is curled up in her LAIR.
The sun is shining with its warm LIGHT.

I like this nonsense poem, even though
all the sentences are different lenghts
the rhyme pattern ties it all together.

POETRY POWER-UP

See if you can write a new poem using the techniques above but about one theme like night-time? Or dreams? It can be about absolutely anything!

11

TAKE YOUR PEN ON A JOURNEY

We are going to take our pens on a
journey by doing something called a **freewrite**!

A freewrite is writing whatever comes into your head for a couple of minutes.
It could be a list of words or random thoughts that don't have to make sense.
You could even write, "I don't know what to write," again and again until other
words come. You could look around the room and list or describe what you see.
You could close your eyes and write what you can hear… people scribbling, feet
shuffling, people breathing, a bird tweeting. Anything goes in a freewrite!

1. Are you ready? Set a timer for 2 minutes. Ready… Steady… **WRITE!**

TIME'S UP

2. Underline anything that you like from your freewrite.
It might be a single word, a sentence or an idea.

3. Looking at the words you've underlined see if you can make
a poem out of them. Maybe you can mix them up to make a poem,
or add some more words to connect them together, maybe one
word will spark off an idea for a whole new story.

POETRY Power-up

For an extra challenge see if you can freewrite for longer
than two minutes. Add a minute each time you do a freewrite
and see if you can end up writing for 5 minutes, non-stop.
What poetic worlds will you discover?

Meeow!

Oink!

ONOMATOPOEIA

ONOMATOPOEIA. It's a big word! But it just means words that are sounds.
Easy examples of onomatopoeia are animal sounds. A duck makes
the sound ***QUACK***, and so we've turned the sound into a word.
A dog ***BARKS*** and that sound has become the word... ***BARK!***

1. Make a list of all the different animal sounds you can think of, I'll start you off...

Woof   Quack   Meow

2. Once you have added to the list, try writing sentences where
different animals make the sounds you have listed, for instance:

A dog goes meow.
A duck goes moo.
A cat goes woof.

You can make your sentences as long or as short as you like...

I heard a cow and it went WOOF.

or

I passed a giraffe in the zoo and it went ROAR.

3. Or they could make different noises altogether!
See if you can write five of your own sentences with surprising sounds,
to make a **Surprising Animal Sounds Poem**!

Moo!

POETRY POWER-UP

Squeak!

Quack!

For an extra challenge see if you can add a repeating line
to your Surprising Animal Sounds Poem like this...

The day the animals swapped voices
I heard a cow and it went WOOF.
The day the animals swapped voices
I heard a mouse and it went ROAR.
The day the animals swapped voices
I heard a tarantula and it went MEOW.

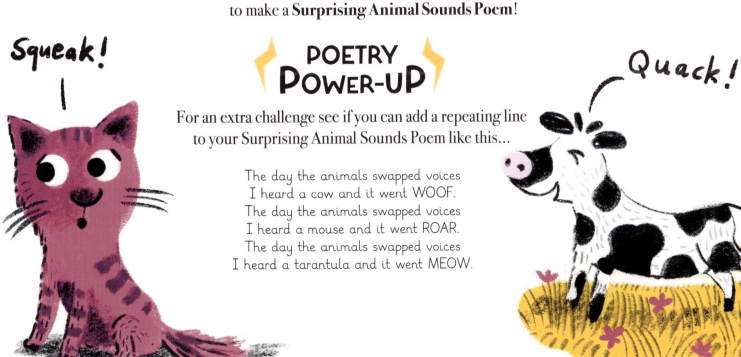

DIMINUENDO POEMS

If I ever get stuck for an idea of what to write about, it often helps to think about how I would like to perform the poem. One technique that I like to use is called **diminuendo.** This is when you start a poem with a loud voice and then get quieter and quieter.

What do you think would make a good subject for a poem that starts loud and then gets quieter? Maybe a poem about a baby crying and then being soothed by a lullaby? Or a poem about a factory with all its clunking machines. Bit by bit the machines get turned off as everyone goes home.

Here's my poem about a ride from the city into the countryside...

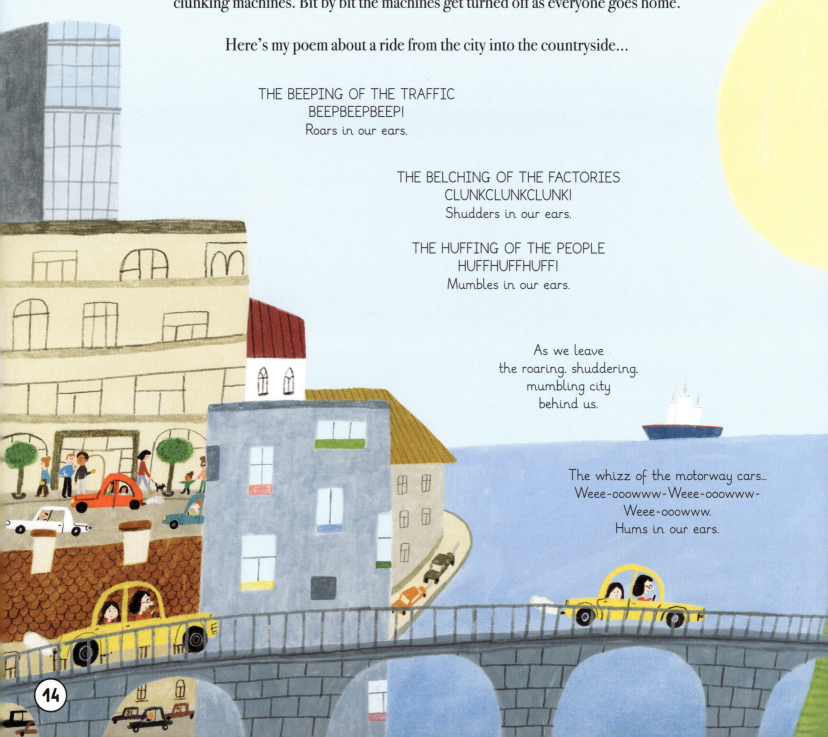

THE BEEPING OF THE TRAFFIC
BEEPBEEPBEEP!
Roars in our ears.

THE BELCHING OF THE FACTORIES
CLUNKCLUNKCLUNK!
Shudders in our ears.

THE HUFFING OF THE PEOPLE
HUFFHUFFHUFF!
Mumbles in our ears.

As we leave
the roaring, shuddering,
mumbling city
behind us.

The whizz of the motorway cars...
Weee-ooowww-Weee-ooowww-
Weee-ooowww.
Hums in our ears.

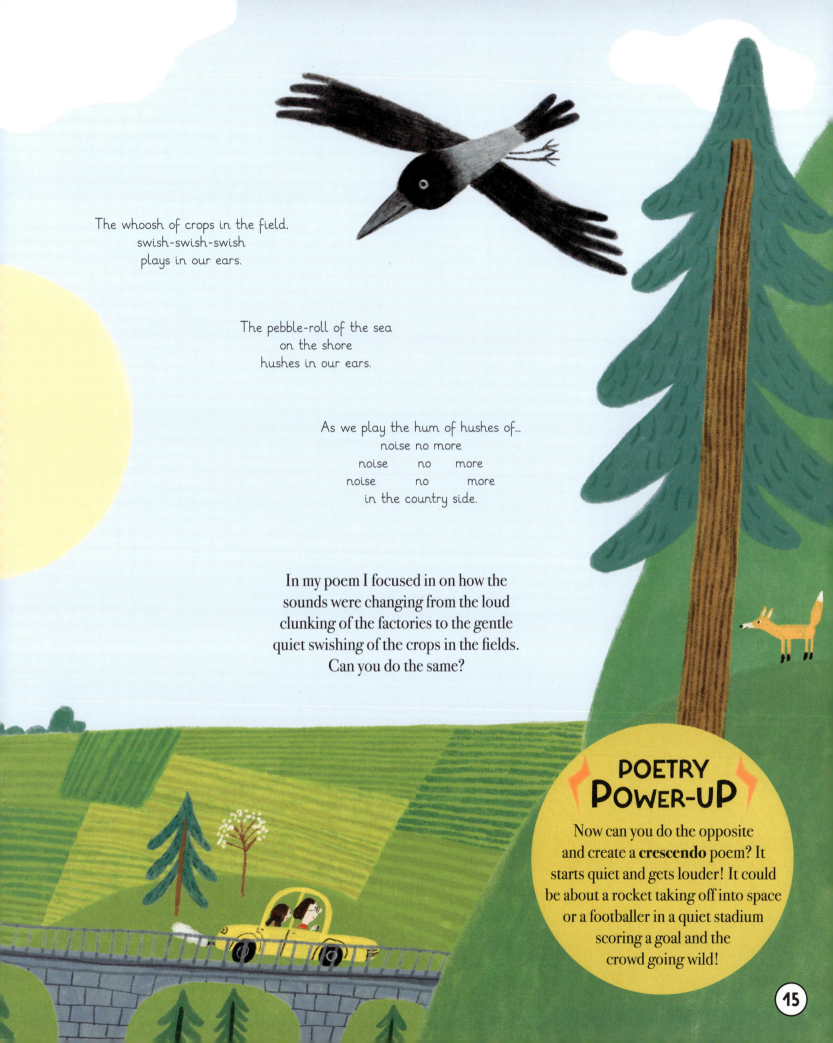

The whoosh of crops in the field,
swish-swish-swish
plays in our ears.

The pebble-roll of the sea
on the shore
hushes in our ears.

As we play the hum of hushes of...
noise no more
noise   no   more
noise   no   more
in the country side.

In my poem I focused in on how the
sounds were changing from the loud
clunking of the factories to the gentle
quiet swishing of the crops in the fields.
Can you do the same?

POETRY POWER-UP

Now can you do the opposite
and create a **crescendo** poem? It
starts quiet and gets louder! It could
be about a rocket taking off into space
or a footballer in a quiet stadium
scoring a goal and the
crowd going wild!

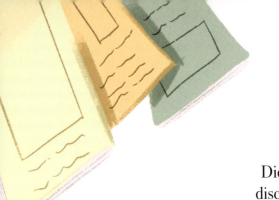

BLACK-OUT POEMS

Did you know that poetry is all around us just waiting to be discovered? I'm going to use some leaflets and junk mail and turn them into poems... **black-out poems**!

1. A black-out poem is really easy to do. All you need is a marker pen. Black permanent markers work best, but you can use an felt-tip or colouring pencil or anything that can black-out a word. Choose a leaflet and look for words and phrases you like the sound of and black-out everything else.

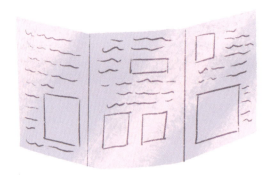

2. Decide which words to keep by looking for connections between them. This way, the bits you leave can make sense on their own. Remember this is poetry, so it doesn't have to make sense. You might just like the sounds of the words you leave. You might like the images the words bring to mind, or maybe the words make you smile, or laugh or even cry!

And that's it – easy, right? You can make black-out poems out of anything with text on it, you can even photocopy pages from books you like and use them. How many poems will you find cloaked in cards, masked in menus or living in leaflets?

POETRY POWER-UP

Take one of your black-out poems and use it a bit like a word bank. You might find that a line sparks off a whole new idea for a poem, song or even a story.

Bug Poem
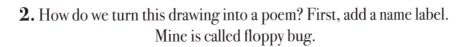

I'm going to show you how you can
turn a drawing into a poem.

1. First, take a sheet of paper and draw your bug! It can be any size or shape you like. Its body might be round, or spiky or made up of lots of parts. Add whatever you like, legs, antennae, eyes, wings, pincers or claws. Then, colour it in with pencils or felt-tips.

2. How do we turn this drawing into a poem? First, add a name label.
Mine is called floppy bug.

3. Next add what the bug eats. Mine eats roasted carrots and pancakes.

4. Finally, add a label saying where your bug lives.
Mine lives in my oldest pair of socks in my sock drawer.

5. Now let's turn these labels into a poem. First, say where the bug lives, then say what it eats and then I will repeat its name three times like this...

"Living in my oldest pair of socks.
eating roasted carrots and pancakes –
A floppy bug
A floppy bug
A floppy bug."

POETRY POWER-UP

Draw and write three more bug poems and add them together. You could even add your poem to your classmates' or friends' poems. How long can your poem get? Remember these are your bug poems so your bugs can be as strange as you like.

SOUNDS OF THE ENVIRONMENT

Let's create a poem about the environment. **A poem inspired by listening**!
I've written one and it goes like this:

From my window
I can hear the rustling of the trees.
From my window
I can hear the sighing of the wind.
From my window
I can hear the rumbling of the cars.

1. I was inspired by looking out
my window and listening. I started
by making lists of the different
sounds I could hear like…

Rustling   Sighing   Rumbling

2. Then I put those
words into sentences.
Why don't you have a go?

POETRY POWER-UP

For an extra challenge see if you can make
your poem rhyme, like this:

From my window
I can hear the CREAKING of the TREES,
It sounds like music in the summer BREEZE.
From my window
I can hear people TALKING,
having a little chat, talking and WALKING.
From my window
I can hear a man SINGING
his voice is beautiful like a bell RINGING.

Halloween poem.

Imagine there was a club for werewolves.
I wonder what the rules for this club would be?

Here is my **poem about the rules** for Werewolf Club.

Werewolf Club Rules

DO NOT run to Werewolf Club
You can bound to it in moonlight
but never run.
DO NOT bring silver to Werewolf Club
you can bring meat... red meat...
but definitely no silver.
DO NOT bring cats to Werewolf Club
you can bring rats and bats
but definitely no cats.

How did I write it? I started it with three '**Do nots**',
followed by a silly rule for each one.

Write out a list of '**Do nots**' in your notebook and complete them.
How wonderfully weird can you make your rules?

POETRY Power-up

I wonder what the rules would be for Vampire Club,
Zombie Club, or even Loch Ness Monster Club.
Why don't you have a go at writing them.

WAYS TO DESCRIBE COLOURS

This poem paints a rainbow, but it doesn't mention a single colour by name!
Can you guess what colours I am talking about in my **colour poem**?

> The first of the colours
> is a poppy flower,
> a drip of lava,
> a flame's hot power.
>
> The second of the colours
> is a bumble bee's bright stripe,
> a daisy's laugh,
> a banana just ripe.
>
> The third of the colours
> a dragon fruit blush,
> a kitten's cute tongue,
> an embarrassed flush.

Did you guess the colours? They are **RED**, **YELLOW** and **PINK**.

When I wanted you to imagine yellow, I wrote about yellow
things such as a bumble bee's bright stripe and bananas.
I made you to think about the colour without naming it.

1. Now it's your turn – think of your favourite colour.
Make a list of things that are that colour, like this…

Red

Fire engine, roses,
post boxes,
clown noses,
apples, Mars

2. Now try using your word list to start writing
your poem, starting with the line:

The First of the colours is...

3. Then complete the sentence using some
of the items from your list to describe the colour.

4. Repeat the process with some other colours and remember
that the starting line changes a little bit each time.

Here is a poem I've made using my list:

The first of the colours is
a fire engine.
a blooming bright rose
a clown's apple nose.

5. You could stop at three colours and have a three verse
poem like mine or you could keep going, adding more
and more colours until you have an entire rainbow.

POETRY POWER-UP

Read a verse of your poem to a friend and see if
they can guess which colour you are talking about. If they guess
correctly then they can read you a verse of their poem. Keep going
until someone has correctly guessed all of the colours.

SIMILE HUNT

Do you know about **similes?** They are simply when you use 'like' or 'as' to compare. For example 'My smile is **as** bright **as** the sun', or 'I'm angry **like** a lion'.

Hamster! Hamster!

We've got a hamster in our class,
as brown as toffee.
He's so sweet, so cute,
with chubby cheeks
for storing nuts and fruit.
He sips from a water bottle
strapped to his cage
like a little baby!

Awww, he's soooooo cute.

He's got these darling little paws,
like a doll's hands
and a sweet, cute, tiny little tail,
like a little piece of spaghetti!

Awww, he is sooo deliciously cute.

One day I put my finger up to his cage,
and he sniffed it with a nose
like a chocolate chip button
and he... BIT ME!

We've got a hamster in our class,
as brown as a bog.
He is so mean, so horrible
with fat cheeks
for storing pupils fingers.

He sucks at a water bottle
strapped to his cage
like a greedy rat!
Ohhh, he's sooo mean.

He's got these vicious claws
as terrible as a tiger's
and a long wiggerly, squiggerly tail
as scaly as a snake!

Arrr, he is sooo perfectly horrid.

Did you spot the similies?
Sometimes when I'm writing, I don't know what to write.
When that happens I go on a **simile hunt** to get inspired.

1. Similes are all around us. To go on a simile hunt you will need some
sticky notes and a pen. You can do the simile hunt inside or outside.
Look around you notice the colours and textures, sights and sounds.
You might see a leaf on a plant and think...

The leaf is as green as a dragon.

You can write that on the sticky note and stick it to the plant.

You might see a wall and think...

The wall is as hard as rock.

2. Once you have five or more collect them up, stick them onto
a piece of paper and reorder them. Which simile should go first in
your poem, which should go second... which should go last?

POETRY POWER-UP

Once you have decided the
best order for your similes,
try writing them out neatly.
Add some extra lines, these
can be more similes or totally
different lines to connect
the similes up.

POEMS TO BE READ FAST

Whenever I get stuck, I think about how I would like my poem to be performed. If I want a slow poem, I write about falling asleep, or swimming in jelly. If I want a poem read super-fast, then I think about **speedy themes.**

Speedy Rocket

This rocket's going fast!
        Super-fast!
Faster than light,
        it's out of sight!
        A zipping zapping rocket
                on a slip stream trip
    it rides
        it rips
    through the Milky way it dips!
    It whips,
        it slips,
                meteors it clips!
    It zips,
        It tips,
    this rocket shakes its hips!

This super-duper-blooper rocket
    sliding on a beam of light
it's bright, a fright, it swerves incredibly tight.
    This rocket's so wonderfully fast.
    It arrives at night-time before night!

It's a dream-exploding,
    mind-imploding
zooming melody of thought-dissolving,
whizzing cacophony of engine thrust
    it's time revolving!
An incredible super speedy rocket ship!

What do you think would make a good subject for a poem being read **FAST**?
When you have come up with some ideas you can start writing your poem.

POETRY POWER-UP

Now think about a good subject for a poem
that will be read **SLOWLY** to help the listener feel relaxed.

WRITING ON STONES

Have you ever written on a stone? It's a lot of fun all
you need are some stones and a permanent marker.

My days are hard,
I have heavy thoughts
the stony sky is grey
but that is my favourite
kind of weather.

Did you notice that I used some stone related words in the poem
like **HARD** and **HEAVY**, **STONY** and **GREY**.

1. Another way to write poems on stones is to use smaller pebbles and to write one
word on each pebble. make sure you leave some blank (you'll see why in a moment).

2. Put all your pebble words in a bag, jumble them up and pour them out.

3. Look at how the pebbles have landed to get inspiration for sentences.
If you are missing any words you can fill them in on your blank, unused pebbles.

Your pebble poem might be random or make sense it might be magical
or about something everyday, it's up to you.

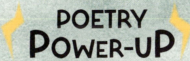

POETRY POWER-UP

Get a friend or family member to create their own bag of
pebble words and take it in turn to spill your bags and
create some poems. You could swap pebbles or combine your
sets to come up with some super-long pebble poems. If you
can, take a photo of your pebble poem to remember them.

TURNING SIMILES INTO METAPHORS

Let's create a little poem using **metaphors**.

1. First of all, think of a simile that uses **like** or **as**.
What do you think the sun is like? Write down as many similes for the sun
as you can in one minute. Here is one of mine:

The sun is like the eye of a dragon, it is as hot as lava.

2. Now we are going to turn this into a metaphor just by taking out the words
LIKE and *AS*. A metaphor is just when we say something *IS* something else.

The sun is the eye of a dragon, it is hot lava.

3. Now add more lines to make the writing really pop.
Think about your metaphor, what other details could you add?
Could you describe smells? Sounds? Tastes?

The sun is the eye of a dragon,
it is hot lava,
burning bright,
heating the ground
until smoke rises
and tickles my nose.

I have broken the lines up, when I do this it is called a
'line break', line breaks make a poem look like a poem and you
can put them wherever feels right to you.

POETRY
Power-up

Write four more poems that turn a simile into a metaphor and make each one about a different season. One for spring, summer, autumn and winter. Here are my season poems:

SPRING is like a hug

Spring is a hug

Spring is a hug
that warms and comforts
as new blossoms bloom.

SUMMER is like
a volcano erupting

Summer is
a volcano erupting

Summer is
a volcano erupting
spreading its heat
in lazy days
as insects buzz and swarm.

AUTUMN is like
a firework display.

Autumn is
a firework display.

Autumn is
a firework display
with leaves of every
fire-burst colour.

WINTER is like
a polar bear.

Winter is
a polar bear.

Winter is
a polar bear
roaring its cold
around us.

What will you do with your poems? Will you read them to your class?
Write them on an old water bottle with felt tips and hang them in a window?
Maybe you could write them in your poetry notebook from page 7?

EMOTION POEMS

Let's create poems using our faces and our **feelings**.
Poems about feeling happy, sad, nervous or excited.

1. Have a go at pulling faces for different emotions:
happy, sad, confused and angry.

2. Write down how those faces made you feel.
Did pulling a sad face make you feel like you were eating cold porridge?
Did pulling a curious face make you feel like your brain was full of light bulbs? Did pulling
a nervous face make you feel like you had springs attached to your knees?

Here's a poem of mine inspired by pulling an angry face:

> When I'm angry
> my body is rock,
> my face is wet clay.
> Meteorites inhabit my fists,
> my voice is all smoke and fire.

and here's another inspired by pulling an excited face:

> When I'm excited
> my toes are ants,
> I'm a river bubbling
> and an air current of wishes
> my smile could explode the sun.

3. Have a go at writing your own emotion
poems. Remember to start by pulling a face,
thinking about how you feel and put it all in
the poem. It can be as strange as you like,
you can't get it wrong this is your poem.

POETRY
Power-up

Turn you emotion poem into a riddle. All you have to do is make sure you don't use the name of the emotion in your poem. Read your emotion riddle to a friend and see if they can guess which emotion you are talking about.

Can you guess what this poem is about?

My cheeks feel like rose buds
my tummy glows with sunlight
my shoulders are a forest breeze.

Any ideas? (The answer is at the bottom of the page).

Happiness

MY FAVOURITE FOOD

I love food. All sorts of food, hot food, cold food, spicy food, sweet food...
I wrote this poem all about my **favourite foods**.

Little bit of food

A little bit of rice.
a little bit of pea.
on my plate for my tea.

A little bit of jam.
a little bit of toast.
In the morning's
when I love it most.

A little bit of banger.
a little bit of mash.
in my belly
for a tasty bash.

A little bit of curry.
with a poppadom.
tastes great but it burns my bum!

A little bit of fufu.
a little bit of stew.
eat with your fingers
that's what we do.

A little bit of food.
on my plate.
eat it all up
feeling great.

1. What kinds of food do
you like? Try writing a list of them.
In my poem I use the repeating line
'A little bit of...'.

2. Use your list to complete the sentence 'A little bit of...'.
Here is an example I've written, mine rhymes, but yours
doesn't have to.

A little bit of lamb curry with some rice
I like to eat it, it's very nice.

3. Then add more lines and build up your poem.
Here is my poem. I've separated the different lines
into verses to make it look more like a poem.
These are called 'line breaks' and you can add
them wherever you think they fit or sound right.

A little bit of lamb curry with some rice
Piled up in a great big bowl.

A little bit of ice-cream with some jelly
cold and wobbling in my mouth.

A little bit of mushy peas with some chips
hot and steaming in my hands.

POETRY POWER-UP

For an extra challenge, if you didn't
make your poem rhyme, see if you can make it
rhyme. If it already rhymes, take the rhyme away
and see how long you can make it. Can you get
to five verses, six verses... or TEN?

Reading Aloud in Different Voices

Poetry comes to life when it's up on its feet. When you sing the words of a song you are singing the **lyrics**. We get the words lyrics from ancient Greece, when poems were read to the sound of an instrument called the lyre. So, lyrics are poetry read to music.

1. Poems are meant to be read out loud. Choose a poem you have written or one by someone else and read it out loud!

2. Move around the space you're in while you're reading, being very careful to look where you are going! Moving can help you to feel the words in your whole body. You can read loudly or quietly it's up to you,

3. As you read, experiment with reading in different voices, try an angry v**oice**, a **relaxed voice**, a **happy voice** or the **voice of a robot**!

POETRY Power-uP

Once you've practiced reading by yourself try reading out loud to someone. It might be one person, or a whole room of people. Play around with different voices and discover just how fun poetry can be.

OBJECTS WITH VOICES

Let's bring the contents of your pencil case to life!

1. First of all choose something in your pencil case and really look at it, is it an old and worn eraser? Is it a pencil case filled with lots of zips and secret compartments? Now imagine the object was a person! What kind of person would it be?

Here's one I created about my favourite pen...

> I'm a smooth talking
> funky looking
> silver streamed
> writing machine.
> I am an artist.
> words flow through me
> like rivers.
> I'm never seen without my lid hat.
> I love being snug in a pocket.

What we've done here is called **personification** which is a bit like magic: by giving objects voices we give them personalities and bringing them to life. Have a go at giving a voice to your chosen object.

⚡ POETRY ⚡ POWER-UP

Why not try giving voice to something bigger? Write a poem that personifies a car, an aeroplane, a house, the sun, or even the moon! I wonder what personalities these massive things will have?

WHISPERING POEMS

Thinking about **how a poem will be performed** can be a great way to find inspiration. If we know that the poem is going to be whispered then we can think of subjects to suit whispering. Perhaps it would be a little bit spooky or about secrets. Or maybe its about a baby falling asleep and not wanting to wake them!

Here is my creepy poem, designed to be whispered:

Don't Look Now

Don't look now
don't move, don't breathe
there's something behind you
unlike anything I've seen
it's looking
right at you,
eyes hollow as night
it's pointing its long fingers
its mouth wants to bite.
It's moving its grey lips
so horribly slow
the words it is saying
,, are whispered and low.
Don't look now
it's incredibly near
don't move a hair's width...

It's whispering in your ear!

1. Now it's your turn to create your whispered poem. What do you think would make a good subject? Here are two ideas to get you started...

Think of a secret superpower no one knows about you... what could it be?

Come up with a spooky description of a ghost or monster. What do they look like?

2. When you have an idea you like, you can start writing. Remember there is no right or wrong to poetry it's about having fun with words.

POETRY Power-up

Whisper your poem to five or more people. You could even have a friendly competition with your friends to see who can whisper their poem to the most people! Good luck and happy whispering.

HAIKUS

Haikus are three-line poems.
Traditionally, they are about nature
but they can be about any little moment
like eating your favourite meal.

Haikus have a certain rhythm because there
is a pattern to the number of syllables in each line.
Syllables are the number of sounds in a word or line.
The word as-sem-bly has three syllables.

In a haiku the syllables of all the words in
the first line add up to 5,
the second line adds up to 7 and
the last line is 5 again.

I love beans on toast (5)
warm buttery beans on toast (7)
small. sweet perfect beans. (5)

Pandas are so cool (5)
Big and fluffy gentle bears (7)
They munch on bamboo. (5)

Now it's your turn! Write a Haiku about
your favourite food or animal, or something
totally different. If you find your sentences are
too long or too short, try out different words.
Count the syllables until you get a sentence
that is the right length.

POETRY POWER-UP

Write three Haiku's about water: one could be
about rain, one could be about swimming and one
could be about drinking it. Or you could do three
haikus about three different areas of water like a
pond, a river and a swimming pool!

PANCAKE DAY

Whenever I eat pancakes I like to...
Sprinkle sugar on them.
Roll them up.
Squeeze some lemon over the top of them.
Prick them with my fork.
Cover them in chocolate spread
Slice them into slivers
Stuff them into my mouth
Lick my plate clean

I used lots of **action words** here. Action words are called verbs. Can you think of 5 actions you do when eating pancakes? Then we can turn them into a poem. These are the 5 words I'm going to use:

Cut   Pour   Salivate

Prick   Gobble

When Dad makes pancakes I start to SALIVATE.
I POUR maple syrup all over them.
I use my fork to PRICK each steaming pancake.
I CUT each one up into tiny squares.
And I GOBBLE them up!

POETRY POWER-UP

Let's turn this pancake poem into a **tanka poem**. A tanka poem has a set number of sounds, or syllables in each line. The pattern of syllables goes like this: 5, 7, 5, 7, 7

Pancakes make me drool (5)
I pour syrup over them (7)
I prick with my fork (5)
I cut them up nice and small (7)
And I gobble them all up! (7)

I've had to shorten some lines and make others longer. Counting syllables has forced me to get to the heart of the poem. I can almost taste the pancakes now!

TONGUE TWISTERS

I love **tongue twisters** they're so much fun to say and write...

She sells seashells on the seashore

Peter picked a peck of pickled peppers

Betty Botter bought some butter

Notice anything about these tongue twisters?
Most of the words start with the same letters so if we want to
write our own tongue twisters all we need are lots of words
that start with the same letter. This is called alliteration.

Try

Try twisting your tongue
then tuning your teeth,
try taking your tonsils
from a tummy-tickling thief.

Try tasting your tears
then trumpeting your toes
try taping your temper
to the tip of your nose.

1. To write a tongue twister, start by making a list of words
that start with the same letter. They can be about anything.
A great tool to help you with this is a dictionary.

Here's my list I decided to write lots of
words starting with the letter P...

pancake

plop

party

panic

pit

pear

pairs

partridge

people

Pluto

pebble

pantomime

panda

Peter

plummet

2. Now, add your words into sentences. I'm going to have fun with how the sentences sound, it's going to be a nonsense tongue twister...

Peter has a party pancake shop.
Pairs of people plop into the pit.
Partridges and pandas eat pebbles.
Pluto plummets into a pantomime.

That tongue twister is super-random, but I love it, and it's made me think of lots of weird and unusual things like pancake shops and pandas eating pebbles! Notice that not every single word starts with the letter 'p', just most of them. Have a go at writing your own tongue twister!

POETRY POWER-UP

See if you can write a tongue twister that makes sense. It might take a little more time and you might need a few more words to give you more options for different sentences, if you get stuck finding a word you can use a thesaurus to see if there are any words with similar meanings that start with the letter you need.

I flew a paper plane over a pond
the people paddling watched it pass
I pelted a pebble at the plane
It plummeted down with a plop.

WORLD REFUGEE DAY

World Refugee Day a day set by the United Nations. It honours those who have been forced to leave their home country because of conflict or persecution. Refugees don't choose to leave their homes, they have to because their homes are no longer safe. Often, they have no idea if or when they will return. Let's think about what home means to us. Here's my **home poem**:

Home Is...

Home is more than a door
more than a roof
and the walls of a building.

Home is the way the sunlight
filters through my bedroom window.
Home is a hello from my neighbour
and the smiles collected in my local shop.

Home is knowing the seasons,
knowing the sky,
knowing the day will be calm.

Home is cuddles with my cat,
and races with my dog.
Home is my favourite brand of cereal
and knowing which shops have it.

Home is the walk I take after dinner,
past my favourite tree,
and the grassy hill
where the daffodils pop in spring.

Home is having a map
to family and friends,
always knowing where to find them.

When I was writing my poem I wanted to think about all the things that make my home, home! I realised it's more than the bricks of the building, it's a sense of place and familiarity. It's the people and the sights and sounds.

Write your own home poem. You can use the repeating phrase 'Home is...' and then simply describe the different things, people, pets, sights and sounds that make your home unique.

Writing this poem can help us reflect on the courage and the bravery of refugees. It can help us feel empathy. Empathy is getting an idea of what it would be like to walk in someone else's shoes. When we feel empathy and when others feel empathy for us, the world becomes a kinder, safer place. Where we all recognise our shared humanity and where no one need feel alone.

POETRY POWER-UP

Read your poem to someone else and ask them what home means to them. See if you can find three similarities between your ideas of home and together turn these three similarities into a poem you create together. For this new poem you could use the repeating phrase 'Our homes are...' Good luck and happy writing.

EASTER TRIOLETS

When I think about Easter I think of
Easter eggs. I've written a poem about my
excitement when finding sweets inside an Easter egg!

A   I wonder If I'll find sweets inside?
B   The egg starts to crack as I bite.
a   the chocolate melts. I go goggle-eyed.
A   I wonder If I'll find sweets inside?
a   Some sour jellies to make me tongue-tied!
b   I widen the crack with another bite!
A   I wonder If I'll find sweets inside?
B   The egg starts to crack as I bite.

This eight-line poem is called a **triolet** and it's very simple to write.
Even though the poem has eight lines, five of those lines repeat!
When writing a poem like this, we can use labels
to help us understand the pattern. That's what the letters
on the side of the poem are for.

The first line of the triolet is repeated three times on the first,
fourth and seventh lines, labelled with a capital A.
The second line is repeated twice on the second
and the eighth lines, labelled with a capital B.

We use little letters 'a' and 'b' for non-repeating lines that rhyme.
The little 'a' lines rhyme with the capital A lines
and the little 'b' line rhymes with the capital B lines.

And that's what
makes a triolet!

POETRY Power-Up

Copy the letter pattern below. Fill in the gaps to write
your own triolet about anything you like: your
favourite computer game, an imaginary pet or
what you'd like to do as you grow older.
The more triolets you write the more the structure of the
poem will become second nature. Before you know it,
you won't have to write down the labels, you will just
know how to write a triolet!

This line needs → A   This line is
to rhyme with   B   repeated
this line → a   here
   A
   a
   b
→ A   and here
   B

Repeating a line

One of the easiest ways to create a poem is to think of a line
and repeat it throughout your poem. When I was a kid, I was always
told to take off my shoes when I came home to our flat. So, my **repeating line** will be...

Take off your shoes, Joe! Take off your shoes.

I'm going to add some of the other things my mum
would say in-between the repeating lines, to build up the poem:

Take off your shoes, Joe! take off your shoes.
You're treading mud all over the flat!
Take off your shoes, Joe! Take off your shoes.
I've just mopped the floor!

Take off your shoes, Joe! Take off your shoes.
You've had them on all day!
Take off your shoes, Joe! Take off your shoes.
Inside is not where we play!

Do you see how the repeating line gives the poem a structure?
When I perform the poem I could ask the audience to repeat the line with me.

I have made the last verse rhyme by using the words **DAY** and **PLAY**.
I thought this gave my poem a nice ending.

Now it's your turn think of something you're always
told to do or not do. For example are you always told
to tidy your room? You could even
add in your name like I did with mine...

Tidy your room, Joe! Tidy your room.

Or are you always told to eat your greens? Or to stop playing on the computer?
Once you have chosen your repeating line all you have to do is add some lines in-between.
Think about the reasons why you are told to do or not do something.

My mum would always ask me to take the
rubbish out and I always had lots of excuses...

Take out the rubbish, Joe! Take out the rubbish!
I can't, Mum, I've got homework to do.
Take out the rubbish, Joe! Take out the rubbish!
But Mum, the rubbish stinks!

Take out the rubbish, Joe! Take out the rubbish!
I would but there's a spider in the bin!
Take out the rubbish, Joe! Take out the rubbish!
Can't my little sister do it?

Take out the rubbish, Joe! Take out the rubbish!
Ok, just this once!

POETRY POWER-UP

Write your poem with two voices like I have above,
with a parent or carer asking you to do something,
followed by why you can't do it.
Perform your poem with a friend and bring
this poem to life. You could perform
your poem to your class or family members
or friends, just remember to have fun!

FOUND POEMS

Found poems that are discovered by chance and with a little bit of luck.
They occur where words happen to be near each other: for instance the titles of books
on a bookshelf. Found poems are out there, just waiting to be discovered!

Go on a hunt for a found poem and write it down! Here are two poems exactly as I found them:

In A Library
Eye and Brain
Seeing Things
Opticks
Colour Physics
Vision and Realism
The Eyes Have It.
Beloved
Seeing Stars
George – Don't Do That
The Magic Flute and Other Childrens' Stories
Trickster Makes This World.
Did My Neurons Make Me Do It?
Receptors and Recognition
Solid Clues.
The Days Run Away
Like Wild Horses Over The Hills
Jazz
Energy Flash.

On A menu

Cold-Pressed,
The Lemonade
Pure Green
British Berry
Rise & Shine
Fresh Juices.
Library Food
Snacks
Freshly Baked Pastry
Smoked Olives
Fried Chicken Bites
Fish Finger.

Are there any poems
hiding near you?

POETRY POWER-UP

Once you've written down a found poem.
Try making it longer. Add to it, rearrange it,
use it as inspiration for something totally new.
Here's one I'd based on one of the poems I found
in a library. If you look closely you can see
the remnants of the original poem.

Library Food

A snack of poetry
a bowl of haikus
a packet of chewy sour limericks.
Freshly baked short stories
served hot and steaming.
Smoked novels
mouth-wateringly long.
Fried joke books
Finger-licking good.

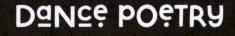

DANCE POETRY

One of the things I love to do is dance, which gives me an idea for a **concrete poem**! A concrete poem is when a poem is written in a shape.

1. There are blue some shapes of dancers on this page. Copy these out big on a piece of paper.

2. Next, fill a sheet of paper with any words or phrases you can think of connected to dancing. Like 'spin' and 'tap' or phrases like, 'their feet are a blur of magic.'

3. Now, copy the words and phrases into onto the shape of the dancers. The beauty of doing it in this way is that we don't quite know how the poem will be. We are simply fitting the words into the shape, and the poem at the end is a surprise.

POETRY POWER-UP

For this challenge, perform your concrete dance poem! You could do this with some friends. One of you could read the lines of the poem while someone else moves like a dancer across the stage, moving in all the wonderful ways that the poem suggests.

RECIPE POEMS

Recipe books are filled with great action words like **BAKE, SIEVE, STIR, BEAT, KNEAD** and phrases like ***A CUP*** of flour, a ***PINCH*** of salt, a ***DASH*** of oil and a ***HANDFUL*** of chocolate chips! This gives me an idea for a poem, what if I imagined **a recipe for me**?

A recipe for me

Take a handful of words
and mix in a bowl.
Add a sprinkle of laughter,
stir until soggy.
Take a pinch of bravery
and fold through the mixture.

Add a cup of sugar-
because I'm very sweet!
Roll out on a sunny beach,
and cut out the shape of me.

Bake in a warm library
until risen.
Serve straightaway
with a pen!

Start by thinking of all the words you've read in recipe books.
Here are some words I've found to get you started. But you might
find more wonderful words in a recipe book you have at home or in the library.

Bake
Roast
Mix
Stir
Sieve
Pour
Sprinkle
Dust
Fold
Grate
Fry
Cut
Cook

A cup of...
A handful...
A litre of...
A dash of...
A Pinch of...

POETRY POWER-UP

Why not add a little spice to your recipe poem by adding alliteration. Alliteration means words that start with the same letter like, 'she sells, sea shells on the sea shore.' Read back through your recipe poem and see if you can add any more words that start with the same letter.

Make Believe Animals

Let's make up some bizarre **poetic animals**. Starting with a verse for the head and then making our way down the body like this...

This creature has a peculiar head
it is covered in feathers
of the brightest red!

This creature has the strangest face
with a nose so long
it can win any race!

This creature has a wobbly neck
composed of wires.
it's very high tech!

This creature has terrible arms
they wiggle and squiggle
and set off alarms!

This creature has delicate legs
thin and spidery.
dancing on eggs.

This creature has baffling feet
with a twist of its knees
its toes become seats!

Each verse has a new rhyme. I thought about words
that rhyme with the different body parts so when I was writing about the creatures
neck, I though of the word tech and that word gave me the idea for the verse.

Have a go at writing your own strange
creature poem using rhyme.

You can use these rhyming words to help...

Head - bed - lead - shed
Face - race - lace - suitcase
Neck - tech - wreck - peck
Arms - alarms - farms - charms
Legs - eggs - pegs
Feet - sheet - seat - treat

 POETRY
POWER-UP

Perform your poem as the creature you're
describing. Change your face and move your body
to bring this creature off the page! You could even
change your voice, mirroring the sorts of sounds
the creature might make.

PHOTO POETRY

Let's turn a photo into a poem!

1. All you need is a large print out of a photo, some tracing paper, paperclips and felt tips. Start by writing a short poem about the photo. My photo is of a ladybird, so I started by writing a list of words that come to mind:

Red
Dots
Black
Ready to fly
Hidden wings
Surprise flyer
As round as a tear drop
Dots like pupils

And this is the poem that the words inspired...

As round as a teardrop
the ladybird waits
with its shell of pupils.
Ready to gaze into flight.
to blink with hidden wings
a blur of red and black.

2. Now you have the poem, write it out again, but this time write it on some tracing paper clipped to the photograph. As you write, change the shape of the words to match the photo. Some letters might be very big and curved!

Don't worry too much about the order of the lines, think of your poem as a palette of words that you are using to create a picture. You can repeat the bits of the poem as many times as you like to fill the picture.

POETRY POWER-UP

Ask someone at home to print an A4 version of an old photo of a special memory. Then write a poem about that time, what do you remember? What did you see? What could you smell? Create your own memory photo poem.

Renga Poems

Renga poems are from Japan and are over 700 years old! They are written
in a group, each person adding a new stanza. A simple way to write one is
to link lots of haikus together. Each time a verse is added it should be
inspired by the verse that came before it, like this:

> The sun is shining
> I try hard to score a goal
> I kick it too hard!
>
> My boot leaves my foot
> sailing high into the sky
> heading for the clouds.
>
> The clouds become dark
> a storm of rain starts to fall
> the river now floods.
>
> The flooded homes drown
> under a deluge of waves
> and a young man's tears.

Each verse is a haiku with 5 syllables in the first line,
7 syllables in the second line and
5 syllables in the third line.

The renga can be as long as you like, some have been a hundred verses long!
You don't have to make yours as long as that and you don't have to do it alone,
the whole point of a renga is that you write it with your friends.
Take a verse each and seeing how long it ends up being.

POETRY POWER-UP

Have a go at writing a renga with your friends about something
that you all enjoy – it might be a sport, it might be a food
or a computer game. Make sure it's something
you all feel passionate about. Good luck!

HEART POEMS

A poem works best when it comes from the heart. Let's write a poem all about our heart and our **feelings of kindness**. I've written one and it goes like this:

When I share a smile,
my heart is filled with candy.

When I learn something new
my heart swells with rainbow clouds.

When a friend asks if I'm ok,
speaking the beat of their heart into mine,
our hearts sing a melody.

When my carer says she is proud of me,
my heart leaps, and twirls and spins.

When my father tells me "well done,"
my heart glows and grows.

When I whisper a kind word to another,
my heart becomes a super hero.

Can you write a poem about your heart and all it feels? How can you put those feelings into words? I speak about my heart being 'filled with candy' and 'swelling with rainbow clouds'. But how does your heart feel? Does it become as soft as puppy fur, or bubbles with joy? To inspire you, think of kind things others have done for you or that you have done for others.

POETRY POWER-UP

Cut a heart shape out of paper and write your poem on it. If you have more than one poem, you could make a heart-shaped booklet. You could make a collection of heart poems from all the people in your class.

ANIMAL VOICES

I love animals and imagining that they could talk, when I think about a lion,
I imagine that if it could talk it would sound like this...

Lion

I am meat-licker.
bone-cruncher.
big-meower.
I cat-walk with pride.
My mane is a hairdo of envy.
My roar is a rumble of mountain.
My claws a savannah of pain.

In this poem I used some **'kennings'**. Kennings are two words joined together which describe something. 'Meat-licker' and 'big-meower' are kennings. When I when I perform this poem, I put on a deep, lion voice.

Frog

I leap. I croak
I am the friend of witches.
I hop. I leap.
I'm often found in ditches.
in ponds.
in lakes.
and even under logs
some say I'm green and warty
but I'm a smooth –
jewel-skin frog.

I perform this froggy poem in a croaky and slow voice – just how I imagine a frog would sound.

Why don't you have a go at creating your own animal poem? You can use some rhyme, some kennings, or simply stick to describing the animal's day. Have a go at reading your poem out loud in the animal's voice. Do you think its voice would be deep or high, fast or slow?

POETRY POWER-UP

Can you create a zoo of animal poems? You could do this on your own or you could work with friends or classmates. What are the penguins talking about? What is the gossip in the spider tank? When you have your poems, perform them, get other people to visit your poetic animal zoo!

ABECEDARIUS

One of my favourite types of poem is an **abecedarius** also known as
an **alphabet poem.** It's very simple and you might know it from when you were little.
The only rule is that you start each line with a letter of the alphabet, like this:

A is for apple
B is for ball
C is for cat
D is for dog

Instead of saying A is for... try writing a more creative abercerdius, like this:

An Abercedarius is just the thing that
Brave poets use to make their poetry sing.
Collect up the letters from A to Zee
Drop them down on a page, it's quite easy.
Find a sentence that starts with each letter
Give your poem a chance, it can only get better.
Have a go at a story or even some rhyme
I used rhyme here to add a punch to each line!
Just see what words come as your pen dances the page
Kindle a poem's fire, let it burn on a stage
Let your lines be long or short or inbetween
Make up your own rules, just say what you mean.
Never fear the poem, let it take you by the hand
Only brave poets will discover new lands.
Ponder each letter and the words they begin,
Query a thesaurus for new words to put in.
Rest assured that these poems can be tricky
Sometimes the endings can get a bit sticky!
Talk to your classmates, help each other find words
Usually the last few letters start to get a little absurd!
Vast vain volcanoes! You see? That was quite offbeat
Wait a minute! For the next letter, I'm going to cheat...
eXamine my technique of using words that start with EX
Yes I cheated but you still get the intended effect!
Zip up your pencil case there is zero to do
your zany poem is finished and was written by you.

POETRY POWER-UP

I challenge you to add some alliteration to you abcedarius. Alliteration is when we use lots of words that start with the same letter. In my poem you may have noticed that I used a few Z words in the last line...

Zip up your pencil case there is zero to do
your Zany poem is finished and was written by you.

Can you do the same for your whole poem adding more
A words to the 1st line, more B words to the second line and so on?
This way we will really be able to hear how you have threaded
the alphabet throughout your poem.

CHRISTMAS

The festive season is a time of coming together with friends and family, celebration and reflection, rest and goodwill.

1. Let's write **a poem to remember** all the cool things you might get up to during Christmas. Start by writing everything down in a list. Here's mine:

Open presents
Wear my Christmas sweater
Eat some Christmas dinner
Chat with my family
Watch some festive movies
Eat some Christmas cake
Go for a walk
Pull a cracker
Tell a joke
Play some games
Laugh until I snort
Write some thank you cards
Have a nap
Play a game
Have an argument
Read a book
Write a poem

2. Now let's turn it into a poem. The simplest way, is by putting a repeating line between each thing in the list, like this:

On Christmas Day
I opened my presents.
On Christmas Day
I wore my Christmas sweater.
On Christmas Day
I ate some Christmas Dinner.
On Christmas Day
I chatted with my family.
On Christmas Day
I recycled my wrapping paper.

Notice how the repeating line gives your poem a structure and a rhythm!

3. If you want you can even extend each line in a verse like this:

On Christmas Day
I opened my presents
I got a surprise gift
a live talking pheasant!

On Christmas Day
I got a Christmas jumper
Not a normal sweater
but a kangaroo named Thumper!

On Christmas Day
I ate all my Christmas dinner
I chomped the sprouts and swallowed the gravy.
I'm the Christmas dinner winner!

POETRY POWER-UP

It's time for an extra challenge, and an excellent way to
recycle some wrapping paper. With a grown up, cut out
a jumper shape. Write a Christmas jumper poem inside it.
It can be about anything Christmas jumper related!

Grandpa knitted me a jumper
of red and yellow and green
a wooly Christmas jumper
with a brilliant reindeer scene.
It had Rudolph on the front
with his bright and shining nose.
it had elves dancing
in the bright and thrilling snow.

NEW YEAR'S RESOLUTION

Traditionally, the start of the year is a time when people make **New Year's resolutions**. They give themselves goals for the year ahead. They could be to read more, to eat more healthily or to write more poems!

Let's write about our new year's resolution but in an **epistolary poem**. That means a poem in the form of a letter. These poems often use more flowery, poetic language. They can be to a person, or even a thing such as a season or a tree. We're going to write a letter poem to our future selves about all the things we hope for in the year ahead.

Dear Future Joe,
I am writing from the past.
Do you remember me?
Sitting on the sofa
with my notebook in my hands
wondering about the new shoots
of the year ahead.

How is the gym going?
Are your muscles like flower bulbs
hard and full of summer strength?
Do words shower from your pen
like April rains,
coating the pavements
of this notebook's final fields
in a rainbow reflecting shimmer?

How have you changed?
Have new skills unfurled
in your fertile mind?
Have you learnt the names
of new summer blooms?

I've mixed my hopes for the year ahead with the language of spring and new beginnings. Words like:

New shoots, flower bulbs, summer strength, April showers, rainbows, fields, unfurled, fertile, summer blooms

These words make up a 'word world' all related to spring, a season associated with change and new beginnings. Word worlds can add texture and layers to our writing.

Word worlds can change a poem completely! Here is the same poem, using a superhero word world:

Dear Future Joe,
I am writing from the past.
Do you remember me?
Sitting on the sofa
with my notebook in my hands
wondering about the new powers I'd gain
in the year ahead.

How is the gym going?
Are your muscles super-strong
and hard, full of laser beams and super-serum?
Do words zap from you pen
like energy sparks,
electrifying the pages
of this notebook's final frontiers
in a cascade of hero pizazz?!

How have you changed?
Have new abilities
revealed their secret identities
in your mastermind?
Have you learnt the names
of every hero you could be?

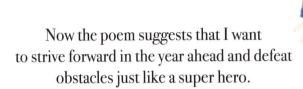

Now the poem suggests that I want to strive forward in the year ahead and defeat obstacles just like a super hero.

1. Now it's your turn. Start by thinking of your word world and making a list of words. You could use the ones I used above for spring or superheroes or something different like the weather:

Sunny, thunder, lightning, storm, breeze, clouds, rainbows, typhoon, hurricane.

Dear Future Joe,
I hope our days have been full of sunny skies...

2. Now all you have to do is write a letter to yourself and see if you can pepper in some of the words from your word world.

POETRY POWER-UP

We've looked at the year ahead but what do you want to do in five or even ten years' time? Write two more epistolary poems as long or as short as you like to your future self's five and ten years from now. What wonderful things does your future have in store?

A POET-TREE

Let's create a **poet-tree!**

From the deep dark earth
the roots rise up
through the mud and slime
and grubs and grime
the roots rise up.

At the trunk of the tree
the roots come together
until they're bound and knitted tight
with a dream of a great height.
The roots come together.

The trunk twists and turns,
spins up from the ground
with blood of sap and skin of bark,
a new wooden statue in the park,
spins up from the ground.

And now the roots that were below
unfurl their branches up above.
They stretch their windings to the sky,
they reach for clouds way up high and
unfurl their branches up above.

This poem describes a tree, poetically!
Each of the four stanzas is about
a different part of the tree.

I chose to repeat some of the lines to give a
sense of rhythm. I also made the third and forth lines in
each stanza rhyme. And just like that,
I made up my own poetic structure.

Have a go at writing your own. How many stanzas will
your poem have? Will each have the same number of
lines? Will some lines rhyme? It's your poem so whatever
you decide is fine, the most important thing to do is have
fun while you're writing.

POETRY POWER-UP

Write out your poem in the shape
of a tree, this is called a **shape
poem**. If you're doing this in
class, you could create
a poet-tree forest!

PLASTIC POLLUTION

We all know that plastic is a problem; it pollutes our rivers and seas. But there is a great deal we can do to help, from joining litter clean-up groups, to using less plastic to recycling. Let's write **a poem about plastic** we have thrown away.

1. Think of three plastic things you have put in the rubbish and one thing you have recycled and imagine where they might be now.

The water bottle I threw away
in a central London bin
rolled from the bin collectors,
was kicked into the Thames
and now floats its way out to sea,
broken down by the sun,
nibbled by fishes.

The chocolate wrapper
that blew from my hands
on a windy playground after school
never came down.
It has circled the world forty times
over mountains and forests
over deserts and jungles.

The bubble wrap that covered
my brand new bike
fluttered from the dump to a field
buried by earth and roots
suffocating the ground.

The plastic bag I recycled
became part of a rucksack,
that carried a student's books
and art projects
and games and lunch
until it, too, was ready to be recycled again.

This poem helps us to think about the waste we create and what happens to it next.

2. It might help to do a little bit of research for your poem about what happens to plastic next. You could think about what it might become once it's been recycled.

POETRY POWER-UP

Get a marker pen and write your poem on a piece of plastic: an old water bottle or an old crisp packet. If everyone in your class does the same you could create a display that will encourage us all to recycle.

HOMOPHONES

Have you heard of **homophones**? They are
words that sound the same but have different meanings.

Homophones are a challenge to use in a poem. But if you're like me,
the challenge makes the writing of the poem even more enjoyable!

Two Knights at Night

In the middle of the NIGHT
two KNIGHTS had a thought
to head out for adventure,
to leave behind their boring fort.

They put their helmets on their heads,
lifted their swords of incredible WEIGHT
t'was the hour for adventure - they yelled,
"Our adventure cannot WAIT!"

These two SONS of once brave kingdoms
rode into the SUN to begin their TALE,
leaping the roots of their route
right into a dragon's TAIL!

It was long, it was green,
as green as a PEAR.
The PAIR readied their shields
and followed the tail to a lair.

The endless winding tail
wound into a cave's endless HOLE.
Skeletons littered the ground,
not one of them was WHOLE.

"Oh NO," said one knight,
"I don't KNOW about this."
"Have no fear," said the other,
then they heard a monstrous hiss.

Two knights were swallowed whole
in a deep and night-dark cave.
The dragon still waits there,
sending the foolish to an early grave.

Did you spot the homophones in CAPITAL LETTERS? Now it's your turn to write your own homophone poem. My poem makes a little story but you don't have to, you can write a nonsense poem using homophones. Remember, it is your poem, and you are the boss.

POETRY POWER-UP

Swap your homophone poems with a friend and hunt for the homophones – how many homophones can you find in someone else's poem? How many can they find in yours? If you like you could even have a competition to see who can cram the most homophones into a poem!

Poetry Prompts © 2023 Quarto Publishing plc.
Text © 2023 Joseph Coelho
Illustrations © 2023 Georgie Birkett, Grasya Olyiko, Amanda Quartey & Viola Wang

First Published in 2023 by Wide Eyed Editions,
an imprint of The Quarto Group.
1 Triptych Place, London, SE1 9SH, United Kingdom.
T (0)20 7700 6700 F (0)20 7700 8066 **www.Quarto.com**

A catalogue record for this book is available from the British Library.

ISBN 978-0-7112-8511-8
eISBN 978-0-7112-8513-2

The illustrations were created digitally
Set in Kocha, Bodoni 72 and School Hand

Designer: Myrto Dimitrakoulia
Editor: Lucy Brownridge
Production Controller: Dawn Cameron
Commissioning Editor: Lucy Brownridge
Art Director: Karissa Santos
Publisher: Debbie Foy

Manufactured in Guangdong, China TT072023

9 8 7 6 5 4 3 2 1